THE DRAMA TOMORROW

THE
DRAMA TOMORROW

by

SIR CEDRIC HARDWICKE

THE REDE LECTURE
DELIVERED BEFORE THE UNIVERSITY
OF CAMBRIDGE ON
18 FEBRUARY
1936

CAMBRIDGE
AT THE UNIVERSITY PRESS

1936

CAMBRIDGE
UNIVERSITY PRESS

University Printing House, Cambridge CB2 8BS, United Kingdom

Published in the United States of America by Cambridge University Press, New York

Cambridge University Press is part of the University of Cambridge.

It furthers the University's mission by disseminating knowledge in the pursuit of education, learning and research at the highest international levels of excellence.

www.cambridge.org
Information on this title: www.cambridge.org/9781107686755

© Cambridge University Press 1936

First published 1936
First paperback edition 2014

A catalogue record for this publication is available from the British Library

ISBN 978-1-107-68675-5 Paperback

THE DRAMA TOMORROW

I choose as my subject "the drama tomorrow".
With a somewhat doubtful appropriateness I
recall a letter sent to me by a playgoer during
the run of *The Apple Cart*, in which I played
the part of King Magnus. The writer, a lady
of obviously penetrating discernment, said that
she did not admire my performance, chiefly
because I did not look or behave much like
a king, though she did think my repartee, in
the circumstances, was quite good. To look
convincing as a king, I wish to say, is not an
easy task, and, in a Shaw play, it is apt to be
a responsibility. At least I shall not need any
one so minded in this audience to write and
tell me that, equally, I am not very convincing
as an advocate of the drama and its future, for
that, too, is not an easy task, while of my
responsibility in trying to interest you even
for a few minutes I am, I can assure you, most
deeply sensible. Having chosen my subject,

I am conscious also of the possibility of there being some among you having doubt of its matching the occasion, for the drama is widely held to have not only no claim to a future but an undistinguished, if not wholly insignificant, present. I take it, therefore, that my first business is to show you why, in my judgment, the drama has a tomorrow and also why I think it worthy of discussion and emphasis in this place.

I begin by assuming, possibly with a rashness certain people would deplore, that human nature itself has a future. Optimism about the future of civilisation—may I say?—happens not to be a factor in my own mental development. But, standing here, for a moment of time I am reassured. And, challenged about the future of the drama here and now, I shall reply that as long as human nature survives the theatre will also survive. The theatre was created out of an inherent human need. I deny that the cinema was so created or that television, if it is really coming, will be. These are novelties. We are discussing, as I truly believe, something with the nature of a verity. The theatre had its beginning in the essentially human desire, deeply rooted, for corporate physical action. In the course of time this desire became crystallised in an ordered ritual, partly mime, partly speech; and from that evolved a more or less passive attendance at these expressions of it. So long as ritual, which, after all, is only vicarious action, is performed, the audience, whether the occasion be a State procession, a religious ceremony, or the presentation of the drama, cannot be entirely passive. Audiences are and must always be an integral part of it, participating in it by their sympathetic reactions. That participation, which is not only a satisfying personal experience but an actual and fundamental human necessity, can be effected only by living contact. It reaches its height in the performance of a great play, which is art made flesh.

This association of stage and religion is neither fortuitous nor casual. It is, I could almost say, profound enough to be recognised as part of evolution. The theatre, as we have often enough been reminded, has its deepest roots in religious rites. So, for that matter, did much else that, with the passing of time, has lost all traces of its first parenthood. Religion and the drama, however, still have a spiritual affinity. As the distinguishing mark of all the religions which have commanded the attention of humanity is some form of reincarnation by which our dreams of goodness have been epitomised in one personality, so the special gift of the theatre is to incarnate men's dreams of beauty and perfection. Every other art is individual, aloof. In solitude you may read a poem, listen to a symphony, gaze at a picture, contemplate sculpture. In each instance the artist communicates with you by means of the materials of which he is the master. But in the drama the material the creator uses is humanity itself, and he makes his appeal not to you or to me as entities but to mankind. He may indeed require all these other arts to render him service in the pursuit of his own art. He calls on the poet for his language, the painter for his scenery, the musician to emphasise this mood or that. But these are the embellishments, not the essence. That consists, as was long ago said, of "three boards and a passion". Together, in just that basic simplicity, author and actor collaborate in the greatest art of them all. For centuries, so, they have moved men's hearts and minds with the agony of Œdipus and the madness of Lear, the doom of Orestes and the bewilderment of Hamlet. So, I believe, they will go on moving them as long as life shall last.

What do we find, for instance, at this moment in history when, according to some of the prophets, the momentum given to the theatre by its greatest writers and actors is clearly slackening? With the disappearance of the touring company, which has been almost completely eclipsed by the celluloid eruption of the cinema, little drama movements are more numerous than they have ever been.

The latest information from the British Drama League is that well over ten thousand groups of people are reading, discussing, acting and no doubt writing plays in the cities and towns and villages of Great Britain. Here in your own town of Cambridge there has opened this week a theatre which, I feel quite certain, will play a conspicuous part in this general reawakening. Someone professed in my hearing to see in all this nothing more than the vanity of the petty human ego. Reading a play, at any rate, strikes me as being a singularly inadequate form of expressing a popular emotion. No; I prefer to believe, as I sincerely do, that this is a powerful symptom of the inner need of which I have spoken.

For my part, if I may assume your concurrence in this argument, I shall willingly agree that the future expression of this fundamental need may quite well involve many changes threatening the physical affinities of the theatre as we now know it with that of tomorrow. But before going on to a brief consideration of them, may we, please, survey the theatre as we see it now. We see a theatre which is damned and darkened by many forces making for its extinction. The prophets of that cataclysmic process have great weight on their side. They bring up their heavy armaments of the cinema, broadcasting, television, and reinforce them with much talk about all these factors being only still in their infancy, with the implication, most marked, of even greater wonders of science to come. Science is cast as the demon king in this piece, as in many another modern tragedy. Science, which has destroyed philosophies, is destroying also the arts; so we are told and, I have no doubt, with a certain degree of realism and truth. It is not a comfortable experience, watching the slow decline of an art form which gave us a Shakespeare. And, after him, Tchekov, Ibsen, Shaw, Sheridan, to name no others, and including no great actors of the parts they conceived. It is poor consolation to be told that the theatre is supplying most of the talent that has gone into the making of the immense moving picture industry. For the time being, indeed, the theatre does appear to be fulfilling the purely architectural and domestic function of "wings" to the great world entertainment stage which the cinema has now become, and we who haunt them are but servants of shadows. And something must be said, I think in melancholy tones, about the effect of these great developments on dramatic art, for never before has the creative artist had so many media at his command. Where is the playwright now who has no thought of the possibilities of adapting his works to the needs of the screen? Where is the novelist who disdains to think and talk, most professionally, of all the different "rights" he has for sale? The industrial and scientific revolution has affected the actor no less. Strange, new words have found their way into his technical vocabulary and often, too, he has a strange, new way of saying them, so that one trembles a little for the future of our English tongue. It all sounds very much like chaos and many would say that chaos it most certainly is. Obviously, the stage has found it hard to survive and justify its survival in a world increasingly hostile to any institution not furthering the cause of "realism" in all its grimmest and most shattering manifestations. The post-war generation of men and women started this demand for "reality" above all things. They demanded that dramatists should show them "life", as if living itself were not sufficiently intense for them. The theatre, their theatre, was not an "escape" for them. They wanted life smeared on thickly. Creative imagination—that was *not* wanted. The world was relaxing. Thinking became unfashionable. But if the theatre challenges life—why, then it is bound to lose. It lost heavily in those hectic years. Noting that fact, it is interesting to reflect on another, which is that since Sir Henry Irving delivered his lecture here on the drama some forty years ago, life and the drama have changed places. At that time the theatre was considered to be slightly disreputable;

parents, for example, were in the habit of forbidding their children to have anything to do with it. Life then, on the surface, at any rate, was colourless. There was no opportunity for reading much about sensational crimes, let us say, or of knowing more than a very little about that mysterious and attractive locale known as the underworld—not unless, that is, one bought a pink publication called *The Police Times*. Family life was dominated by austere men and women; there was a decided rigidity about existence, even, I imagine, on the lowest levels of the population. Any bright light seen to be burning in the gloom was almost inevitably the light of a theatre; and, by the way, the light did not jump about all over the place, as theatre lights invariably do now. Actors were shunned in private life, and grew to be so proud of being different from the rest of mankind that they developed certain hallmarks of their own, including fur or astrakhan collars to their coats, long hair, and absurd, flowing neckwear. They were picturesque, I suppose, if not intellectual. At any rate, it does appear that, in compensation for the relative greyness outside, life within the theatre became excessively gay and colourful. It employed, I believe with devastating effects, all the arts of coloured lighting, of which it held the monopoly. The scenery was sentimentalised and crude to a degree: a simple daisy was wont to measure at least a foot in diameter, while every room represented on the stage would have done justice to Buckingham Palace itself. Colour, sentiment, acting, were all distorted beyond life-size. Today there is more drama on the front page of a newspaper than in the whole of the West End of London. The theatre is indeed a restful place after the St Vitus display of the lights of Piccadilly Circus, and, I would add, there is frequently more make-up in the stalls than on the stage. The theatre is now thought to be almost academic entertainment when compared with the frankly commercial appeal of the cinema. There are parents who consider it part of the education of their children that they should be taken to the play. Actors have cut their hair, taken to patronising the best tailors, and gone into Society, and, I may add, as quite possibly you have every reason to observe, they have not gained in intellectuality what they have lost in picturesqueness.

It is the theatre that has become austere and coldly critical of life today, while that life moves farther and farther from the Victorian scene into a world that seems to grow more colourful, more brilliant, more frank, and, speaking with one eye on the Continent, more dramatic. The actor's voice has dropped from the declamatory to the almost confiding coo of the crooner, and his gestures are restricted to lighting a cigarette or putting an offending corner of a handkerchief discreetly into its correct place in his jacket pocket. So that now the strain of comprehending a play is thrown entirely on the ear which, because of the absence of adequate gesture, is put to an increasingly severe test. Acting has given way to behaviour and tends to become inarticulate. Scenery is so factual that we scarcely notice it. I should say that there is more acting nowadays in a motor-car showroom when a potential customer enters, and certainly more at the average business interview, than there is in the modern theatre. Perhaps we have arrived at a time when only the worst actors aspire to the stage. The cleavage between the theatre of yesterday and that of today is wide and deep. In the drama of yesterday the audience found relief from the repressions of life outside. Today free expression is to be found in life, while the drama is suffering from acute repression. Not only the actors and scenery are involved; there is the type of entertainment. The call for realism split theatrical production into two divisions. On the one side we had the attempt to *satisfy* the would-be realists; on the other, spectacle—two kinds of entertainment which can be evolved with infinitely greater effect through the medium of the cinema. During the period in which the stage was vainly competing with life, the film scenario-minded people came in and showed that they could achieve that end much more successfully. Van Druten and Sherriff, for instance, held the mirror up to Nature in quite a remarkable way ; few there are among us who have not met the characters in *London Wall* and *Journey's End*. But they are characters that can be still more convincingly portrayed by the film. The "action off", which on the stage is made as real as possible by conventional tricks, can be shown in its entirety on the screen; there are few difficulties, either of time or space, which the film producer cannot overcome.

But when the drama is lifted to an imaginative level its scope becomes even wider than that of the film, for so long as the imagination is set alight by fine acting and fine writing, the action of a play can encompass anything. The battles in the Greek drama described by Messengers are far more satisfying than Hollywood's reconstructed marchings and countermarchings. For this reason Shakespeare and other dramatists of the time when the theatre was not bound by realism will never be suited to film representation. What planner of spectacle could hope to realise for the audience Macbeth's castle, as described by Shakespeare, or to satisfy it as to the beauty of Prospero's island so completely as does the text of the play? These plays were written with the purpose of converting a bare stage into a rare and beautiful setting. Photographed poetry is like a song illustrated by lantern slides in our childhood—inadequate, not to put it more strongly.

The difference between the modern dramatist and Shakespeare—and it has been stated often enough—is that the modern dramatist tends to demand less from his audiences; there are critics who do not scruple to say that he does not even demand intelligence if he can help it. The Nature which Shakespearean audiences expected to see in the mirror of the stage was the nature of their own emotions;

what today we should call, I believe, psychological reactions. Hamlet will survive the most thorough scrutiny by expert psychologists. As a "case" he is perfect; everything he does in response to this stimulus or that can be checked with similar cases today. He would be a bold prophet who declared that Shakespeare will yet be the salvation of the theatre. But I submit that one must respect the inspiration of any such claim. For what is it that keeps, even now, several thousands of people—in no wise are we comparing them with the cinema's hordes—faithful to the traditions of the stage? If I reply to that question: Because the theatre possesses "just that little something the others haven't got", I run the risk, I fear, of being charged with a lack of responsibility on a vital occasion. I admit that I have not found it at all easy to express what I feel is the right answer to the question. The Americans are fond of terming it personality. There are people who would speak of it as having something or other to do with mental harmony. The ancients called it art and had done with it. Like all things that are hard to describe, it has many names. Perhaps telepathy is one of them. But even when the matter of personality, call it what you will, is left out of the discussion, the stage does continue to represent an event in the lives of those who support it. Going to the theatre is a real happening, a remembered oasis in Time. You do not look down the years and say, with noticeable enthusiasm, "That was the night we went to the pictures." But you do hear people say, "Ah! that was the evening I saw Irving in *The Bells.*" The easier it becomes for any one and every one to go to the cinema—and today eighty-five per cent. of those who do go pay sixpence or a shilling for their seats—the less likely it is to make an impression or to remain as an experience. That is *not* human nature. It seems to me that the time will inevitably arrive when it will be no more exciting to go to see a film, to listen-in, or to look-in, as I suppose we shall be saying in a few years, than it is to draw a glass of water from a tap. A crude comparison, you may think, but not, I suggest, altogether out of focus, and certainly not one that is ever likely to be made in connection with the theatre. Consider the difference between going to the theatre and going to the cinema. At the cinema you are introduced into the place of entertainment by an attendant, usually in some indistinguishable but notoriously odd disguise, waving an electric torch by means of which you are enabled to squeeze your way past a dozen pairs of extraordinarily reluctant knees, while the chief "star" of the evening woos your attention in exactly the same way, by doing precisely the same thing that she is doing in Hong Kong, Melbourne, Cape Town, and undoubtedly Stockholm. On the other hand, in the theatre the leading lady's exclusiveness to the comparatively small and usually better-mannered audience of which you are a unit is not the least of the factors making for your enjoyment of the experience. Her personality is not insulated from yours by unimaginable quantities of celluloid. There is always that incomparably thrilling chance that she may see *you* there in the stalls and give you one of those glances that may lead to your reviewing your entire life and wondering whether something ought not to be done about it. You had no great difficulty, anyhow, in getting to your seat, even if it was not the acme of cinema comfort when you reached it. And you were dressed, of course, as against merely having your clothes on. It is pleasant to get away from what George Gissing called "the livery of the laborious week". What is more, if your imagination runs to it, you could amuse yourself by noticing what other people were wearing, an occupation in which some people, I believe, find considerable satisfaction. You could take part in the play, in the sense that you could give to it your own intelligence and receive back as much of the author's, the actor's, and the producer's, as each had put into it. Greatly to be thankful for was the fact that you could laugh, if you wished to, and yet not have the mortification of realising that, having laughed, you had missed the very next words spoken on the stage. And in the intervals you could sit back and say just what you liked about the play and all concerned in it, or perhaps listen to what others were saying. All of which, I contend, constitutes a charm and an attraction which no mechanical amusement can ever give any one. The fact is that from its earliest days the theatre has been a social event, and this alone has been a bulwark against its dissolution, especially, I think, in these last more difficult post-war years in which realism had almost driven art and its traditions out into the street. But I do not hold that the theatre will live merely because it stands for a social event in the lives of playgoers. If that were so, various well-defined social trends of our time might very reasonably be employed against me. I believe that the mechanisation of amusements is driving the stage back to the point at which dramatic art started. We have seen the same process in outdoor life in which the excesses of speed have led to a resuscitation of walking and cycling. The human mind, I am tempted to propose, can absorb only so much science, and when the pressure becomes too great there is a reversion to the simplicities. That is why I think that the theatre will move towards its more elementary forms and that the audiences of the drama of tomorrow will be called on to co-operate with the actors, as in the days of Euripides and Shakespeare. The so-called ultra-modern production, in which no scenery is used and in which the audience is asked to fall back on its long-idle imagination, is in reality the oldest form of presentation. Except for lighting effects, modern invention and science have done nothing of value to the theatre of itself, which is not to deny that both have played a great part in providing the means by which audiences are brought to the theatre door. Otherwise, I think all that science and invention have done is to force producers to regard their work as an art form or suffer the penalty of being smothered out of existence by mechanised entertainments. I believe this co-operation of the audience with the actors on the stage, of which I have spoken, will be a highly important factor in the future of the artistic development of the drama. It is not unlikely to go even farther than it did in the earliest days and it will undoubtedly bring about a revolution in the mind of the theatre-going public. An interesting example of how much an audience is capable of appreciating this co-operation was afforded by the recent production of the play, *Young England*. The play, in itself not to the taste of most playgoers, would probably have been taken off inside a week had not the audience decided to enter into the spirit of the thing by "heckling" the players, calling out certain of the lines in unison with those required to say them on the stage, and keeping up a running fire of comment generally. In fact, everybody thoroughly enjoyed the piece and the evening, with the result that the play swept into a considerable commercial success. There was no question here, I need not say, of a genuine attempt to break away from the traditions of reality and spectacle. We find one such attempt, and a successful one, in the revival of an ancient Chinese play, *Lady Precious Stream*, in which the scenery is of the most elementary kind. The keynote of the whole production is simplicity, so that we find a pass over mountains represented by two men holding a sheet of canvas. The dialogue is simple and nearly in the earliest tradition. After all, simplicity appeals to the human mind and, with the gregarious habit that man seems not at all disposed to shed, I think it is bound to ensure the continuance of the theatre, regardless of the trend of science and invention. On the Continent these so-called modern productions are common and popular. Russia, always ready enough to break away from any link binding the people to the West, has revolution-ised its stage. Shólokov and Okhlópkov as-sume, without affectation, that their audiences are quite prepared to co-operate with the actors in their plays, which are designed to conceal from the audience things which it is essential to conceal from the characters in them. If the audience knows where the body is hidden, why do not members of it tell the detectives? So runs the Russian argument.

An exceptional example of this type of play is *The Aristocrats* by Pogódin, which tells the story of anti-Soviet prisoners being converted by hard work and careful propaganda into decent citizens of the State. The play is to be regarded by the audience as an event on the stage, not a performance of a play at all. It is even suggested that if the audience were to come into the theatre ten minutes after the play had started even the least intelligent person would still be able to follow, and appreciate, its progress. It is claimed that the audience might be watching, as it were, some drama in the street and that, as watchers, they would form part of it. The stage employed is in the

(28)

form of two large bagatelle boards and there are neither footlights, curtains, draperies, nor special lights. There is nothing to divide the audience from the stage.

And here it would appear that the stage is attacking the cinema at what is probably its one vulnerable point. It is not possible for the audience in a cinema to co-operate with the shadows on the screen. A good many of us can remember a time when silent dramas of the Wild West were being played out before our young eyes on the screen and when we shouted our warnings to the heroine who was riding nonchalantly up to the cactus clump that concealed the cattle rustlers who were the cause of all the trouble on her father's ranch. But it was pretty poor fun; we all admit it. Another advantage that I think the stage may claim is that it is possible for the actor to give his audience what I can only describe as individual attention and treatment. The point here is that every audience is a different one; you will find no affinity, beyond their interest in the production, between the audience of Monday night and Saturday night. Actors, if they are great actors, are masters of mob psychology. The greatest actors the stage has known were completely independent of the material with which they were provided. They had the power to magnetise the public. The more brilliant the actor the less important the background against which his personality shone. I have known it to be suggested that Garrick or Kean or Irving would inspire only laughter by their performances today. I cannot controvert that suggestion. I can only say that in my belief they would not be lost for long, that they would soon dominate the crowd. Once, some years ago, I watched Madame Sarah Bernhardt playing to an audience in a provincial music-hall here in England. It was a disrespectful audience; I do not imagine that many people in it had heard of the great actress. The play was in French and they soon became restless, for her powers were in decline. It was not long before they were rejecting the play *and* Sarah Bernhardt, with a bitter emphasis that only an English audience can apply in such circumstances. Shaken for a moment, Bernhardt stepped forward, right out of the action of the play, and began to recite with a passion and a force that in two minutes held the audience completely spellbound. This art, which enables the player to feel by instinct the state of mind of an audience and to dominate it, will be rediscovered. Applied, as I believe it will be then, that is to say, within the action of the play, it will be a restorative power productive of the greatest good for acting and the drama. I suggest, also, that beyond the practical participation by the audience in a play, there is the intellectual appeal, which is really nothing more than co-operation of another and deeper kind. The stage and poetry were at one period so intimately connected that it was out of the question for an actor to speak in prose. Shakespeare's uneducated and peasant characters were some of the first in history to throw poetry aside and to speak in lines without obvious metre. This was not an attempt at achieving realism on the part of Shakespeare, but merely his way of establishing what he conceived to be a true impression of the types he wished to represent. But there are signs, and most interesting ones, that poetry may return to the stage. Much of Mr T. S. Eliot's *Murder in the Cathedral* is pure poetry. Poetry implies purity of diction, and by some it is held that this is where wireless comes into its own. The B.B.C. Shakespearean productions have been most impressive, certainly far more so than those of Hollywood, which, it must be remembered, have at least introduced the poetry of the English language to a world-audience. But as with the cinema, so with the B.B.C.: there are factors of the human personality that are incommunicable by any method of science, and in the case of these twain the audience is denied them. The theatre of tomorrow will be an oasis in a desert of mechanised pleasure. Spectacle and realism will go on being delivered to the people in tin boxes from Elstree and Hollywood. The theatre—*that* will be for beauty.

Beauty! It is a word which, in this age of increasing din, is beginning to sound just a little unreal. Or does my ear deceive me? I wish I had thought of it before, and so imposed less on your time and attention in trying to give expression, with an inadequacy of which I am only too fully aware, to these fugitive thoughts on the theatre and what seems likely to happen to it. For, after all, I do believe with all my heart, that in the word "beauty" is to be found the kernel of the meaning and mission of the theatre in the world of tomorrow. I submit, along with my gratitude for the patience you have shown one whose powers of self-expression are limited to giving expression to the thoughts and ideas of others, that with the encroachment of modern life on the human personality, with the impact of scientific discovery on its privacy and elementary right to peace and quietness— a right which, I was told the other day, only the rich can now be certain of enjoying—we shall rediscover a passionate need for the theatre. It will be a retreat for those who delight in hearing the human voice at its best, who appreciate the charm and distinction of good manners and notable deportment, and who are responsive to the appeal of all that is implied in the term "good taste". Only in the theatre, it seems, are these graces likely to live on: only in the theatre too, I think, shall we find portrayed those patterns of human character at its most majestic that are in themselves an inspiration to a greatness which seems conspicuously lacking from the contemporary scene.